so too have
the doves
gone

so too have the doves gone

reflections
on the theme of conflict

Jardine Press Ltd 2014
www.jardinepress.co.uk

© individual authors 2014

ISBN: 978-0-9565495-8-7

Title taken from 'Mosque in Kabul' by Antony Johae.
Cover image of La Maison Forestière by Simon Patterson/Syndicat d'initiative, Cambrai, France
Design: Catherine Dodds
Images by students of the Fine Art Department at Colchester Institute
www.colchester.ac.uk

Acknowledgements

We wish to thank the following individuals and organisations for their support for this project. Without their interest and enthusiasm, the production of this anthology would not have been possible.

Stephen Boyce (Editor in Chief) who generously gave his time to choosing the poems for this anthology

Vivian Whelpton

The Suffolk Western Front Association for their generous financial support

The Wivenhoe Localities Fund for generous financial support

Belinda Farrell and the **Essex Book Festival** for generous financial support

Lee Pugh, Manager, and staff of the Minories Gallery, Colchester

Jane Frederick and **Claudia Böse** of the Fine Art Department, Colchester Institute of Art

Peter Kennedy and **Poetry Wivenhoe**

Pat Bloom and members of **Mosaic**, Colchester, for financial donation

We are grateful to the poets who contributed to the anthology and to the students from the Fine Art Department at Colchester Institute who found inspiration in the poems for their art work.

We are extremely grateful to **Catherine Dodds** who brought such patience and skill to the design for this book.

Pam Job and Judith Wolton

Contents

Now we are just things hurled...

How dare you flap your raggedness...

For horseflesh, lead and leather
And the broken-shafted cart...

We're fighting for something.
I'm fighting for you...

His missing leg eats kidneys for breakfast...

Postscript

Artists

Artists whose work appears in the anthology can be contacted via The Fine Art Department, Colchester Institute www.colchester.ac.uk

Artist	Poem
Jane Badley	*Praxis*
Jacqueline Bakowski	*How Things Are*
Ruth Fosker	*The Paper – from The Tale of Miss Potter and the Mushrooms*
Sarah Gray	*Rain*
Ruta Grigaite	*Bitter Fruit*
Maria Medina Inglesias	*Landgirl's Song*
Sarah Lidster	*The Bends*
Judith Lunn	*Earth*
Arlene Machin	*A Ballad of 2014*
Kate Owen	*A Joinery*
Sharon Rawlinson	*No Peace Without War*
Abigail Ryman	*No End of a Lesson*

Preface

The inspiration for this Anthology of poems arose from our connection to the Wilfred Owen Memorial in Ors, Northern France, designed by British artist Simon Patterson. It is built around the original Maison Forestière where the poet Wilfred Owen spent his last night. The Memorial's intention is to remember Wilfred Owen and the men who died with him, while celebrating poetry itself. Funding for the project was co-ordinated by Artconnexion France. We were honoured to be invited to the inauguration of the Memorial in October 2011 and to be included in discussions about future use of the performance space.

Following on from this, we decided to produce a poetry anthology based broadly on the theme of 'conflict'. As members of Suffolk Poetry Society, Poetry Wivenhoe and Mosaic (the Colchester Stanza of the Poetry Society), we invited contributions from poets from these Essex and Suffolk based groups. Individual poets from elsewhere, associated with our societies, also contributed and we invited the Winchester poet, Stephen Boyce, to edit the anthology.

Serendipitously, we had been impressed by an exhibition of work at the Minories Gallery by students of the Fine Arts Department at Colchester Institute. Using their chosen media, students had responded to the words of the landscape writer, Robert Macfarlane. Taking this idea of art created from text, we approached Jane Frederick, Head of the Fine Arts Department who, together with her colleague Claudia Böse, enthusiastically agreed to collaborate with us on the Anthology, inviting their students to interpret a selection of anthology poems visually. Illustrations appear in the text of the anthology, other art works will feature in an exhibition at the Minories Gallery, Colchester, for the official launch in March 2014.

Our hope and intention is twofold: that this Anthology will make a contribution to the commemoration of the centenary of The Great War, 1914-18, and will fulfil the original inspiration behind the creation of the Wilfred Owen Memorial, that it should celebrate poetry.

Any profits from the publication will go to Poetry Wivenhoe to support live poetry in the community.

Pam Job and Judith Wolton

Introduction

The theme of an anthology should act as a loose binding, holding in one sheaf poems that are diverse yet have a coherence containing some definition of truth. Often the universal themes best fulfil this function, and what, sadly, could be more universal, timeless or timely than the theme of 'conflict'?

It was a privilege to be asked to choose the poems for this collection. It came about through the selection of one of my own poems for the beautifully produced anthology, Poetry Wivenhoe 2011, following which I got to know Pam Job and was invited to read at Wivenhoe alongside the talented Alex Toms. What a sparky outfit they are at Wivenhoe, going about their business with real flair and imagination. So when Pam invited me to become part of the editorial team for this project it felt like an ideal opportunity for creative collaboration between Essex and Hampshire – and a perfect fit with the inaugural Winchester Poetry Festival, of which I am a trustee.

Reading the poems, I was immediately struck by the range of voices and the variety of interpretations of the theme. Because it is taught so widely in schools, most of us have some experience of the poetry of the First World War, and the influence of the war poets can undoubtedly be heard in some of this work. But so much else is also happening, the collection seethes with learned allusion, social comment, unexpected locations or points of view, the poems variously reflecting feelings of outrage, sorrow, regret and fellow-feeling; they deal with the political, personal and social, the contemporary as well as the historical.

Making the final selection was a daunting task and I sympathise with those whose poems didn't make it on this occasion, but if readers find in this loosely gathered crop, fruits that satisfy or seeds that grow, our job will be complete.

My sincere thanks to the poets and to Pam Job and Judith Wolton for making the task so pleasurable.

Stephen Boyce
Winchester

Now we are just things hurled...

A Joinery

Against a stubborn nail a stubborn hammer pounds,
crushing steel in angles where a straighter steel stood.
Blow on blow on strident blow, this persecution sounds
echoes of its violence forever in the wood.

Great noises end with silence, the hammer's put away,
but what is bent by savagery can never be made good.
Though violence passes finally, this monument will stay:
a nail firmly planted here, forever in the wood.

Oliver King

Rain

So let the rain beat down, as it does, it always has done,
not gentle rain that drops from heaven

but more a weapon, intimating deluge, spearing from
lead clouds in strikes that fall and penetrate

our raw, basic flesh. Our warm clothes are nothing.
This wind and rain dismiss such shields,

lifting our weak feet high, and bullying
us into walls. We become as useless as umbrellas.

I'd always stayed inside in weather like this,
kept safe and dry until it pounded past like an army.

We are faced with our bare stupidity, our saturated skin.
I thought I had a place. We were stuck together.

Now we are just things hurled, a bit of me there,
a bit of you there, and we don't know where we will land.

Joan Norlev Taylor

Fault Lines

Most of us
will always hate you – all of you –
because
we know that some of yours
have done away with some of ours.
And though a few of us
have paid too few of you
in blood
it's nowhere near enough
for any one of us
to start forgetting
what there is to hold against
those of you still left.

Each last one of you,
whatever you pretend,
knows you'd really like
to wipe out all of us:
but only some of us
will come right out and say so.
And now there's one or two
among us going soft:
they want to let you off –
the lot of you –

for all the things
the rest of us will find a way
to settle with you for, one day.

So first we'll deal with them.

Michael Bartholomew-Biggs

Tribe

We are children of the wind.
We travel gently on our mother's arm
keep rhythm with her breath
and murmured song.
Only when we must, we hasten
proud, emboldened
by our father's open-throated roar.

We are brothers to the sand.
Being many, we can claim a space
and hold it by our shifting
weight of numbers.
Our feet tread lightly, make no prints
to walk behind us:
owning all, we leave the landscape empty.

We are not alone.
Those others
always haunt the corners of our eyes
but at a distance, where we try to keep them.
They have tried to tighten borders round us.

They are made of mud
and dung;
are pale, soft-skinned and have short-sighted eyes;
consume spiced rotting foods, not fresh tough meat;
and crouch confined in one another's smells.

Their dwellings foul the ground,
like droppings
left to dry. They hide their sluggish, heavy
bodies from the sun and cold. Their minds
inhabit worlds where words change shape like dunes.

We lay no lines
across the pure and proper curves of earth.
We borrow ground while they
relinquish none
of what they occupy *as well*
and not *instead*.
If we meet, we meet as enemies.

Michael Bartholomew-Biggs

No Defence

To bring an errant bride back to her husband
Achaean armies aimed to take on Troy.
Ten years of siege and then a stratagem;
a hollow horse to gain the city's gates,
the Trojans' trophy – cause for celebration!
Their nemesis, Achaean sword and spear.
The Greeks set fire, avenged and slaughtered, but –
once they'd reduced the topless towers to ruin
few of their fabled force saw home again.
Let's speak to Agamemnon while we can!
O King of Argos, you were in command.
What hidden counsels bred this expedition?

Look, this wasn't about a conspiracy or a lie,
a deception or a deceit. It was a decision.

'Pontius', ventured Procula, 'at the trial
this morning of the Jew, I heard that you
had asked a slave for water and a towel.
Now tell me why you had to wash your hands.
I warned you of my troubled sleep and dream,
the terror that took hold of me that you
would condemn a man with goodness in his soul.

You could see that he was innocent, so why
be party to this callous plot to kill him?
Who were you working with? The Jewish priests?
Conspiring with King Herod? What is truth?!!
The Emperor will hold you in derision!

Look, this isn't about a conspiracy or a lie,
a deception or a deceit. It's a decision.

A misty moon sheds light on Moscow's streets.
French troops seek bread and shelter where they can.
No Russians are abroad, no-one to bow
and bring to Bonaparte the Kremlin's keys.
Moscow is captured, but the victors have
nowhere to go but straggle back to France.
Through snow-blown wastes and ravaged fields,
burnt villages and countless refugees,
some twenty thousand out of half a million
will make it home. How was Napoleon,
the undefeated master strategist,
persuaded to pursue this doomed ambition?

Look, this wasn't about a conspiracy or a lie,
a deception or a deceit. It was a decision.

Peter Sandberg

Praxis

I have stood in overgrown queues for bread.
I have waited in snow and ice and rain.
I have prayed for the dying and the dead.

I have ached for a son's return in vain.
I have looked into the lifeless eyes
of the living, seen the strong insane.

I have heard – believed – too many lies.
A silence weaves each day and night,
ravels and knots our collective cries.

It begins with hunger, a bloodless fight,
the courage of mothers, daughters, wives,
the city domes and their dying light.
I have lost – have lived – too many lives.

Karen Dennison

Guilt

With his arms wrapped
around my waist,
I schlepped for miles.
He grew long legs
to drag behind us
– we were always looking back
to the last stumbling block,
the last big hurdle.

I couldn't shift him,
this surly teenager,
sulking in my shadow.

Day after day,
I braced myself
for the long walk,
hauling my anchor.

I could cope with
the physical:
the private ache of bones
grating against muscle;

but he showed me
old men, left in their beds to rot;
children, with ribs like cages;
bodies, piled like flood sacks;
young men, standing proud,
with guns like trophies.

Lastly, he took
a knife and showed me
my own heart,
shrunken but still ticking;
my intestines,
wound like a noose;
he showed me my kidneys,
curved like grenades:
he pressed one into my palm,
showed me the pin
and walked away.

Rosie Sandler

Outlander

V

When the peace came,
It brought a roar
And me, staggering home,
Smiling at faces
That claimed me as their own.
'He has forgotten,' they whisper.

But I remember
– Especially at night,
When I can't see their eyes:
Things you must run from;
Things you must run towards;
Things you must step over –
Even if they scream your name.
I remember green, the stench of it
And how a head looks
When you crack it open.

I remember how darkness tears at your eyes;
How the pain gets so bad,
You climb inside it.
I remember the roar,
The cold like splinters,
The hunger gnawing
At your bones.

I remember a young boy,
With hope in his eyes,
Who lost them both;
A man with a finger to his lips,
Slipping back into darkness;
A screaming girl, brandishing
Her brother's bloody hand.

I think I remember
What it feels like to die
And to wake,
Weeping, to die again.

Rosie Sandler

The Homecomers

Sometimes out of old stones, out of old pages
There comes the murmur of alien tongues,
Elders on the battlements, voices of other ages.
The palace smokes, the whispering sages
Chirp like cicadas: who cares or remembers the wrongs?

A phantom perhaps, not living girl but dream
Had launched these ships, but phantom ships:
Stesichorus, all men fight for things that seem,
Shadow of glory or ghost with painted lips.

Returning, those who returned,
With strange accents on their mouths
Recalled the tempests, the days which burned
Heart to ashes, flies, disease, scars and growths,
Cramped quarters between the benches, dry rations, squalor,
The mean lie lurking in the cup of valour.

Returning do they recognise
In the banquet hall or derelict shacks
Of a burnt-out village grief or surprise
In what the poet sings?
Or do they turn their backs
For fear the shame should bring
Confusion on disguise,
Blurtings of a beggared King?

Cameron Hawke Smith

How dare you flap your raggedness...

No Peace Without War

Alone in bed with Hardy
far from the madding crowd
I sense before I see you lousing up
the symmetry of curlicues and loops
on meadowsweet- and tulip-papered walls.

O plain brown moth, you wall-creeper,
eye-sucker, ear-filler, solitude-killer,
rug-unraveller, biter of holes
in woollen clothes – how dare you flap
your raggedness inside my paraffin lamp?

Domestic pterodactyl, glass-chimney-clicker,
how can I stop you? I can stop watching you.
Pooff. I douse the flame, close my book
at Hardy's profound ceiling of stars
and drift into a heaven under eyelids.

What makes you throw your horrid suicidal
body at the window? Clickety-thug
and thug again, you blasted hooligan,
some prehistoric memory of flame
must be knocking about in your insect brain.

My grandmother who rests in lucky peace
captured dozens of you with her bare fingers
insensitive to legs on skin or wings in throat
and dropped you in the woodstove. Hundreds of you.
I light the lamp, roll a Sunday supplement

into a weapon of moth destruction.
Ha-bloody-ha, you vermin, I'll get you yet.
You're stupid on the window, I calculate
a whack. Damn. You think you're safe behind
the vine and flower curtain, not a chance.

You stumble to the tabletop, dumb loser.
I trap you under cosmopolitan prose.
Dead moth, you bloodless little dope.
I smirk at your dust on the tablecloth,
nothing wet, merely a brush-away smudge.

Nancy Mattson

A Lesson in Lemonade

Only one grandmother to go and we don't speak,
not since I helped myself to lemonade
and she uncoiled like a cobra.

I think of my father growing up in that house,
the hot poker in his mother's hands,
the fizz on his bare legs.

Suzanne Conway

How Things Are

He is shouting at her in the street,
Shut your Quasimodo mouth,
bitch. She protests, he goes on,
Don't twist and change things.
I'm telling you how things are.

This woman in denim and flowery shoes
just stares.

He empties her purse, counts the coins,
goes off. She says to the ground,
Why don't you believe me?

I want her to go
before he comes back.
But here he comes, smiling,
swinging four cans of Strongbow.

Suzanne Conway

from The Tale of Miss Potter and the Mushrooms

3. The Paper

Imagining what might have happened had Beatrix Potter been permitted to read her paper 'On the Germination of the Spores of the *Agaricineae*' at the Linnæan Society.

You're standing on a stage,
the hall reminding you of a field
after a summer downpour – scores
of pale bald heads are staring at you blankly.
Suddenly you feel
like the blue-coated hero of your tales –
you've been caught trespassing.
Somehow, your female form slipped through the doors
unseen, and now you're trapped in a net of ignorance,
prejudice spreading through the room
like mould along a slice of bread. You clear your throat.

You give your lecture, wait for the applause:
someone coughs, the great clock ticks; silent mirth
hangs in the air, and dust motes dance like spores.

Alex Toms

The Path

For years she trod the hidden path.
Forbidden by both sides,
they'd met in fear;
their hands were words enough.

Now the path's uncovered.
Her hands dig deep into empty pockets.
Her eyes follow the eagle's free-fall
to some prey across the border.

Fran Reader

Bitter Fruit

We live with fear
but hope leaps ahead
as a deer chased by a hound.

We follow the clouded star of hope
and now in the nowhere, claustrophobic expanse
of an East European airport
my older brother, myself, and his friend,
three *bitter fruit brought down to earth,* *
seeking the spring of liberty, *
test out the passports bought at the cost
of two years labour
in dream-filled poppy fields.

We must travel beneath the surface of life
like a frog who takes to the water
to evade the snake ‡ that prides itself
on its venomous power.
We must move without disturbing the sleep
of the coiled serpent whose tongue is forked and jaws are wide.
Our souls live in the silence of our breath. ‡

Fear lays its cold fingered touch on our skins
as we ride on the buffers between bouncing trucks;
steadying ourselves, numb, clasping a cable
while a screaming night express streams past.
We have no light, just the constant glint of steel
swishing and jolting below our feet.
Darkness is the candle ‡ that lights our hope,
non-existence will guarantee our life.

Under tarpaulins on a lorry I cuddle fear close
to keep bottled the fizzing soda of despair
which wants to explode in gulping cries
for my buried mother.

We take our chance at the backs of market stalls
to find a fallen peach, a rolled apple, a coin.
At each border we stick together.
The greatest wealth of this world is the company of friends. *

At Calais we sneak on to the axle of a coach,
hearts pumping but lighter than the feathers of a dove,
blind moles scrabbling our way to England.

No matter how fast you run
your shadow more than keeps up.
Sometimes it's in front. ‡

When authority orders 'come out!', my brother goes first
then I squeeze myself between coach and tarmac.
Reflected in the wide window of the police station
I see passengers on the coach gawping, wondering,
and in the eyes of more than one woman there
the look of my mother when she found me in trouble.

I sink to the ground,
my dreams drained away
with my tears.

Peter Sandberg

* Borrowed from the 20th century Dari poet Ustad Khalilullah
Khalili; Bitter fruit falling upon the earth
‡ Borrowed from the 13th century Dari poet Jalaluddin Rumi;
Enough words?
Both were born in what is now Afghanistan.

Matt Breaks his Silence

Matt has not spoken in four days.
On the first, Maria respected his silence,
offered hopeful glances to his glares,
waited her turn. Simply waited.

On the second, she sparrowed her words
as she hopped from stove to sideboard,
his woman, making his meals on time,
serving them up with gossip and plans,
balancing towards him on the edge of her chair.

On the third, the pleading began,
small at first, then growing larger and more
embarrassing
like a pregnant woman's belly
swollen with purple stretch marks
and a sore-apple navel.
She thrust herself at him.
He turned his head.

On the fourth day.
She bars his exit from their bedroom.
Fills the doorway with her need.
Acknowledge me.
The fist arrives.
She is grateful.
Tastes his knuckles.
Hears the force of the backhand to her ear.
Welcomes his curse.

Nancy Mattson

An Essex Parish

Sigeberht is dead; and there has been a returning...

Sirens burst through the evening hum-drum,
stand me up at my window,
pass as quickly as they come.

Instinct hurries me to the churchyard,
muttering a prayer,
checking my dog collar;

*...there has been a returning from Lamb's blood to the Dragon blood that
bore us, spear point, sword sharp, and fire hearted to Britannia.*

Reaching St Peter's, there's a shadow on the roof,
cigarette glow, moon blue coils of smoke,
my torch fixes to him:

*'you're a lead thief Kyle Goodman.
the police are on their way!'*
But fear is surprised as he gestures me nearer,

descends the drainpipe,
athletic, balletic even, almost dancing,
swaggering towards me, sucking on his cigarette,

just fifteen years old,
a prince in Adidas,
still wearing his first communion face.

*'I wasn't nicking yer lead Vicar.
Mum was with one of her men,
I was angry like I can't explain.'*

He tells me that he broke her windows,
how he raged in rooms steadily emptied
of everything except for the beds,

cursing all the groaning demons of the night,
the semi playful punches that turned to
fag burns and sly kicks, from them

who smiled at his mum and played at father;
and he tells me how this man lay on his kitchen floor
curled-up, whimpering, bloody, foetal,

grasping at the life falling through his fingers.
'I can't remember all of it,' he said,
'but he called for his mother'.

Confession, silence, I recall the canticles
somehow feeling empty,
but move nearer offering a hand.

Sirens again, this time they were close.
He drops a knife into the ground and
turns into the darkness.

> *...and this is Swithelm's Kingdom.*
> *There has been a returning.*

David Canning

Earth

Dry. Cracked.
The soles of their feet. The soil.
Heat shimmers and dust clogs
The cups, bowls, pores and
Settles as black sleep in children's eyes.
She dreams of water, soft silver mirrors
Reservoirs surrounded by grass where cattle grow fat.
And anger, tight, clenched is felt like thunder rising from
the distant purple hills.

Petra McQueen

Kate Owen *A Joinery*

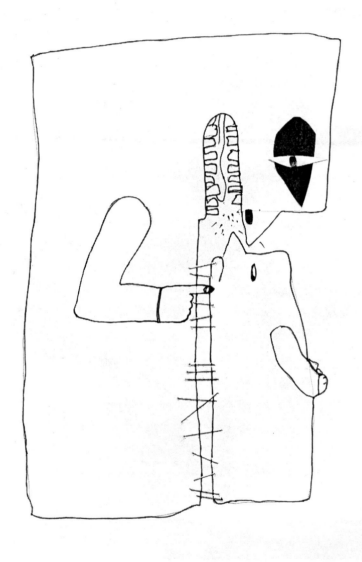

Jacqueline Bakowski *How Things Are*

Jane Badley *Praxis*

Sharon Rawlinson *No Peace Without War*

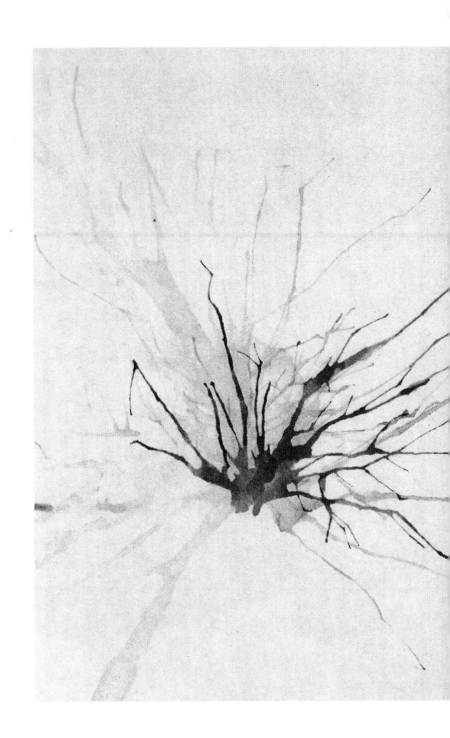

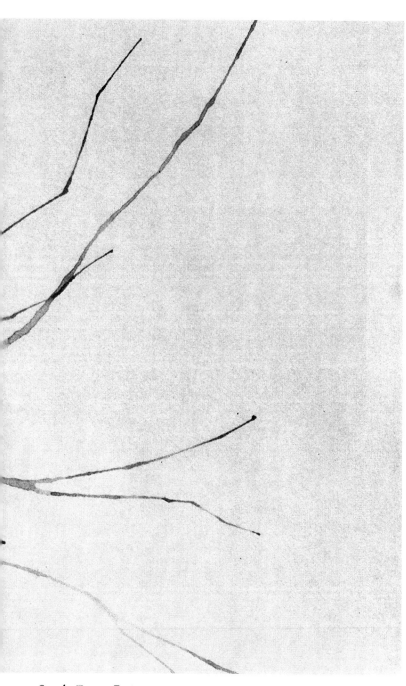

Sarah Gray *Rain*

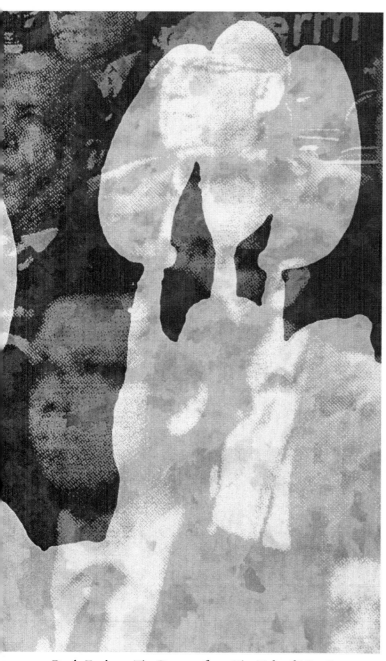

Ruth Fosker *The Paper – from The Tale of Miss Potter and the Mushrooms*

Ruta Grigaite *Bitter Fruit*

For horseflesh, lead and leather
And the broken-shafted cart...

A Ballad of 2014

Shut up about the first world war
Men are still dying and don't know what for
We can't seem to get the point somehow
Shut up about it – end it now

Shut up about that world war one
It's obvious we've not moved on
The last living soldier said it's 'organised murder'
So why celebrate it any further?

And the pity's really not enough
Unless you try to stop that stuff
Mechanical death's an enterprise zone
Click a button, deploy a drone

The officer class is still pretending
The trust they broke won't still need mending
Faking being one of the boys
In their celebratory noise

Nostalgia for sorrow means that you
Have no real feelings that are true
Listen, hear the peacenik say
Goodbye 'Goodbye, Dolly Gray'

Death and horror are bad – we get it
And if war still goes on, you let it
Mostly insulting, sometimes a bore
Shut up about the first world war

Adrian May

Remembrance

For homefires, lions and roses
When the sky was overcast
And the sinew left of England
Turned its back upon the past
And the guns fell quiet at last

For one bird singing sweetly
From fields far beyond
When winter coughed discreetly
In the forest of Rethondes
And black rain swelled the pond

For horseflesh, lead and leather
And the broken-shafted cart
For friends who fell together
And the farmer losing heart
When ploughing couldn't start

For the spectral rails stretching
To the future's gaping yawn
A patient's shaky sketching
And a family left forlorn
For talent never born

For sterling girls and mothers
On clifflands seen from France
For promises to others
When ordered to advance
For the lack of song and dance

For hamlet, town and village
Where lads came back alone
War's ullage and war's spillage
In native blood and bone
Immortalised in stone.

Martin Newell

French Harvest

As we roamed through autumn roads of France
Old Ceres sprawled out glorying in the sun,
Flaunting her ripeness, treading a harvest dance;
Her figs swelling with juice, her hillsides hung
With endless rows of noble, ripening vines.
She offered walnuts dropped from ancient trees,
And sweetest chestnuts flung on country lanes:
She gave us honey from the hives of bees;
Hid mushrooms in the woods for us to find,
And cider apples, tiny, sharp and red.
Up on the coast the oyster growers lined
The bay with seashells shovelled from their bed.

But other fields held ranks of pure white stones
Rising from beds of bullets, boots and bones.

Judith Wolton

Wood at Ors

Leaves in the autumn wood
glow yellow-gold,
translucent; sun strokes
their spines reveals
their veins, warms
them before death.

They hang perilously,
swing like dog-tags,
shiver in the breeze.

Watch!
There are other shadows here.
Shapes drift like smoke
among trees, dark figures
step from charred trunks,
their blackness harsh
on gold.

A boot, an arm, a helmet –
sway and fade at vision's edge.

They were here once, beside
the spring's steel gleam –
breathing for one more night.

Judith Wolton

A Postcard From Flanders

To Thiepval, where the monument
Is sombre as the clouds slouch by,
Standing, squaring massive shoulders
To an honest Flanders sky.
Here the boys of homely counties
Walked one morning in July,
Heard the guns' disastrous gossip,
Listened, then lay down to die.
Here the sons of rainy islands,
Spirits stolen, barely-born
Pals from cobbled towns and cities
Fed these green–blonde fields of corn.
Now the English schoolkids' voices
Echo on impassive stone
Over rolling Flanders farmland
Rich in blood and crumbled bone.

Edwin Lutyen's lines and arches,
Half in tribute, half in mourning,
Etched with names of all the fallen
Loom across the land as warning.
Three or four miles on, at Serre Street
Cemetery Number Two,
Seven thousand souls lie sleeping,
Country traffic trickles through.
In the quietness after passing
Only windsong and the birds.

No amount of grainy archive,
No amount of poets' words
Can prepare the human senses
For the sudden overload
Of the monument at Thiepval,
Witnessed from the lonely road.

Martin Newell

'Literally, For This'

I.M. Edward Thomas

Edward sensed the deepest feelings
as he rose to play his part,
dogged by fear of human failings,
fired by duty to report.

He paid heed to owlish voices,
felt the call to move away
to a place of shattered pieces:
those who fight need not ask why.

As his restless body wandered
through dark trenches of the soul,
Helen must have wept, and wondered
if his mind would ever heal.

Rightly so, for in his letters
Edward spilled the ink of pain:
journal entries mention matters
that would make a loved one swoon.

Feathered comrades on this mission
lived for him in black and white,
bringing solace, consolation,
unaware of pending fate.

Edward's harvest yielded verses:
earth received a loyal son.
All 'for this': his phrase embraces
fertile ground and seed well sown.

Caroline Gill

Moments From a Trench-Career

After Edmund Blunden, *Undertones of War*

(1)
I wasn't eager to go
to the bombing-school near Paradis,
but learned to tramp down muddy roads,
to live in trenches, wash
in a biscuit-tin.

(2)
We stared into confusion.
From the firesteps tried our longest throws
with Mills bombs –
like unlucky boys
whose game of ducks and drakes
turned one day serious.

(3)
Few people on the streets of Ypres,
but the red post-office remained,
advertisements for *Sunlight Zeep*,
for Singer's *Naaimachinen*,
and fragments of the cathedral gateway
where parchment of old music lay
scattered among legless wicker chairs.

(4)
Shells burst around us with a flat
pattering percussion of continual sound.
Then silence, and the solitude recaptured
a wilderness of windowed walls.

(5)
The open space all through the Salient
was crammed with men,
with animals, with transport.
Like a circus-ground.

(6)
Port Arthur where we found
among the broken spades and empty tins
a muddy pair of soldier's boots
– still containing someone's feet.

(7)
Our cheerful young lance-corporal
was making tea that afternoon.
                          A shell
dropped on a sudden from blue sky.
I turned, and when the smoke dispersed
the boy was gobbets of black flesh,
earthwall sotted with his blood.
Bits of pulpy bone. A single eye
stared from the duckboard.

(8)
Another dawn, and rain.
We trudged ahead.
The latest German missile
with a shriek burst over us,
exploded in the mud,
rocked all the earth around,
the very air itself.
My twenty-first year
had come and gone
with mud, and gas,
and high explosives.

Roger Caldwell

Bad Weather: For Isaac Rosenberg

God's castaway, the clumsy clown,
all but a derelict from Cable Street,
he'd known bad weather from the first.
No one denied he had a gift –
though not for living, it would seem..

An absent-minded very raw recruit,
he fought the drizzle and the lice
as much as Germans for his patch of sun,
for summer and the sweeter times
who'd lived in Nomansland already
when he walked Whitechapel streets,
when it was always far, so very far
from here, wherever here would be,
to the British Museum.

Unwritten epics lay beyond the ridge.
They rose before him like the Cambrai spires
glimpsed indistinctly through the mist –
a mist as thick as the tobacco-smoke
that climbed so high above marble tables
to the painted ceiling of the Café Royal.

There is no hope of writing poems now.
Lost in the fog, all his defences smashed,
he falls into a churned-up sea of mud
that welcomes yet another hapless guest,
its April fool, although the weather
shows – too late – some signs of clearing.

Roger Caldwell

Gas

1915, an April day in Ypres –
in what was left of Ypres –
a German rocket-signal flared
across the soaked shell-cratered downland
and a greenish-yellow gaseous mist
drifted on the Belgian breeze
ghost-like over no-man's-land.

It blanketed the ground, flowed over craters,
over rotting bodies of the dead,
through brambles of barbed wire, across
the sandbagged Allied parapets,
seeped into dugouts and deep shelters.

Men who breathed it screamed in pain,
clawed at their throats, stuffed burning mouths
with shirt-tails, scarves, with anything at hand,
tore bare-handed at the mud itself,
then buried their faces in the earth and died,
as the laws of chemistry declared they would.

So much for chlorine. Next came phosphene gas,
spreading across the fields a scent
of new-mown hay, recalling farms of home
to those removed so far from home.
Then in the water-saturated air
it turned to hydrochloric acid, burned
deep into the bubbled tissues of their lungs.

July – and, with a scent of lilac, mustard-gas
that soaked through cloth, dissolved
new-issued rubber masks, and reached for eyes
whose lids inflamed and then swelled shut,
made for fourteen thousand blinded men –

'thus saving countless lives', Fritz Haber said,
'since it will bring war closer to an end.
In times of peace a scientist belongs
to the whole wide world, in times of war
just to his country.' Then swept out
to supervise new trials on the Western Front.

Clara Haber, no less possessed of reason,
herself a chemist of renown, demurred,
and gassed herself.
                        When Fritz returned
he found she'd gone to join the men at Ypres.

Roger Caldwell

Burial

Browngrey chalk clay the earth,
bare the fields the fieldfare breast
fleetingly, as they fare forward north.

A labouring man on his father's ground
this was the browngrey soil he tilled
before he died the first time round,

on an unnamed field of war that became
a black hot diagram of death,
ineradicable in his brain

the disgrace that drove him to hide
his shame, what he thought his shame
at the local asylum, inside,

inside himself where no-one could find him.
And then he died the second time round,
slowly year by year they consigned him –

his family, my people – to convenient
oblivion. He gardened he kept
the lawns, the roses, the lenient

ranks of vegetables, and died
the third time round, a name
only, Irish and Fen, alongside

his people, who will say at last perhaps
there was no shame or if there was
let it lie where it belongs – in our laps.

Irvine Finch b Shelford, Cambridge 1884
d. Fulbourn Hospital 1965

Cameron Hawke Smith

C.O. 1914

'Dear Lisbeth'
(filling in the spaces
on the printed prison form)
'I am well.'

That was all. No
'How is little Enid?
I miss her.
I miss you.'

When he came home,
thin, subdued,
he suffered bilious bouts,
was never the same.

And little Enid,
seven now,
had lost her own Dear Dada
for all time.

Gill Napier

The Deserter

I still remember the day he left,
The day he went and fought,
My son he died a hero,
Or that was what I thought.
My little boy, I raised him well,
He was not born to die,
But his fear got the better of him
And in his grave he lies.
He saw the guns, he turned and ran,
For him this was the end.
My beautiful boy was only scared,
But was shot by his own best friend.

Neave Lynes

*Written in response to a documentary which implied
that a soldier turned back in fear and ran towards
his own guns.*

The Parcel

Mother, open the parcel,
the brown paper's greasy,
it's creased at the corners,
untie the string.

Your fingers are shaking,
out tumbles the crumple
of khaki, or *feldgrau*,
rough-textured and damp.

It lies in your hands with a sigh
and you smother your face
in the fog of its cloth and gag
on the acid of gas

which furs up your tongue
but you hang onto the belt,
its cracked polished leather
dishonoured with mud

and then find the buckle,
still brassy but bent,
it shines out of this mess
that is all we have left.

And look how the uniform clings
as you hold it against you
and then when you drop it,
it folds up like death.

Pam Job

Battlefield

Awaiting shape out there: the battle lines
above the trenches, with the mud, the wire,
at sun up; soon, so very soon.

Frightened by the claustrophobic dark,
cramped men in tunnelled earth redoubts
taste mist over the battlefield,

wait for a whistle blast they dread,
feel the promise in the pre-dawn light,
remember the colours of death.

Terror soaks palms despite the cold;
there's fear of cowardice and lack of faith
yet lust sparks that ecstatic urge to fight,

to stab a rifle in the face of fear and scream
to keep the black dog, Shuck, at bay,
the evil riding on your back.

It seems an eternity this tiny stitch in time.
The thunder of the guns is stilled.
Smoke drifts and eddies settle,

cover the dead, the shattered men
whose visions will not fade. Death has won
some savage calm.

*   *   *   *   *   *   *   *

Scattered gravel, blood and craters of decay
a misty stench and muddy pools remain but
life is there – seeds in dark crevices swelling

into form – hope, earth greening with the
wayward
sun's return; wild wheat and barley grasses,
small red miracles, growing like a breath.

Seasons change, the blood red flowers move on
renewing life, in case we should forget to grieve
for damaged souls who might have died, but lived.

Bryan Thomas

We're fighting for something.
I'm fighting for you...

Letter from Rye, September 9th 1940

'extreme vigilance will be kept tonight as enemy landing likely.'

From the Martello Tower
I watched throughout the night.

At dawn the sea was empty as
a conjurer's hat.

They do not seem to come
but if they do, they'll meet our guns.

We're fighting for something.
I'm fighting for you.

Picture it: a fine domed roof,
marbled with dew; a lantern
throws strange shadows,
spiders creep about the wall.

I was on the beach, the sirens howled.
A hundred German bombers overhead.
One gun spoke, a second gun,
till twenty more
were plugging lead
with a music all their own.

One hit the sea with a fine white splash,
another hit the ground a mile away,
burst into a ball of flames.

If we get through this week,
the end is sure.

Today I saw two wild duck,
contented with their brood of two.

My darling, (may I call you that?)
write again soon.

Anne Boileau

Late Siren: Run for the Anderson

Clutched in mother's arms
flesh warm out of bed
downstairs stumble
through thirties kitchen
night open air
barrage balloons tethered on cables
searchlight sky saucers
low drone aircraft
white wisp cross tracers
ack-ack clean muffled metallic
late siren shrapnel
bursts through apples and grass
tree graze on mother
red orange burns beyond shelter
pyjama rip race
down into Anderson's
freshly turned earth stamped down as floor
musty earth sunken spore odour
rock pebbled mud clumps
clattering on curved roof corrugation
parents
hide blurred emotion
reload composure
a child sees through
eyes suspended in stared vision
in a moment of stillness

distant thrump of shells
dozing on board strips
narrow as boat planks
dreaming of winceyette sheets
Mummy can we
we must wait for the all clear
to walk into the cabbage dark dawn
waiting
glimpse of baked bean tin
innocence burns on the flame rise of candles
in the Boys Book of Adventure
dimly lit faces
of First World War soldiers
trenched in bright smiles
all over by Christmas

Mike Harwood

A Prisoner of War looks at a photograph at Ballast Quay Farm

See, we are leaning on our pitchforks
in the noonday heat –
me, as at home, in a trilby.
Das Kind, Betty, the farmer's daughter
holds the camera carefully,
fresh as the new cut hay
in her cotton frock.
'Thank you,' I say, 'danke,'
and, 'Bitte,' she answers,
as I taught her.

We will walk back to the field
along the lane enclosed by high hawthorn hedges.
On either side small brown butterflies
dance through the hazy net
of pale cow parsley, waist-high,
white campion laced with pink geraniums
and armies of nettles – all shot with thistles
and bright scars of poppies.
Sometimes we stop to stare up above the trees
where a falcon rides warm currents easily.
The only sounds – the scrape and tread
of boots on the rough road
and the hidden birds mingling their calls.

For we do not speak our thoughts –
the rhythm of walking, then of pitching hay
soothes our fears and feelings.
Sometimes a plane drones over.
My eyes flick up and click its shape
like a camera shutter. My heart tightens
And my feet beat hard on the warm earth:
Es - gibt - einen - Gott - und - er - ist - gut.
Es - gibt - einen - Gott - und - er - ist -gut.
There is a God and he is good.

Ann Clarke

Note: The speaker did not return to Germany to live after the
war. He married a local girl and settled in Essex. The other
two men were local farm workers.
Betty Govan, the farmer's daughter, gave the photograph to
the Oral History Project in Wivenhoe. She thought it was
likely that she had taken it as she was always 'messing around
with a camera' as a child, but she couldn't remember clearly.

The Bends

In the safety of a dining room in Kent
the glittering eyes of the Frenchwoman
hold us in thrall; they dare us not to listen.

She is in a concentration camp in the last days of the war.
Lying in the bunk she shares with a woman who's already dead,
she is aware something has changed.
No voices.
No sound at all.
The place bulges with silence.

Softly she slithers to the floor,
shuffles to the unlocked door.
Clutching at the wooden jamb,
she quails at liberty in sunlight.
Her bare soles marry with the grains of grit and dust,
begin to question what this union might mean;
her dead-dull eyes are not yet ready
to engage with those of others that she meets,
the final four of thousands who were brought here.

Songbirds let out of a snare,
the women cautiously explore their freedom.
The kitchen draws them in.
On the table, glistening red, lies a side of beef.
They tear at it with bare hands, eat it raw.

Diana Hirst

Dresden

This city overwhelms me.
Joining the tourist flotsam
eddying at its feet –
I shrink to Lilliputian size –

Frauenkirche, Semper Opera.
Zwinger, Schauspielhaus Theatre –
huge buildings resurrected,
lapped now by modern fripperies –
silver statues, cartoon humans,
rickshaws, guides:

postcards in black and white show
photographs of carpeted destruction,
glory broken, swept by fire.

New baroque looms dark against the sky –
a snub to Bomber Harris.

Too much, too vast.
I find a fountain –
the Cholera Brunnen's
gothic spatchcocked lizards,
shouldered on solid Huns,
spew clean water – celebrate
survival from an earlier plague.

Here it is written:
'There shall no evil befall Thee.'

Judith Wolton

Landgirl's Song

for Dorothea Boggis Rolfe

I press my head into her flank.
She chomps and slobbers on cow-cake.
Milk-jets hiss and froth
into the pail.

Three days we had for our honeymoon.
On Tuesday the moon was full and we
were lifted on its arc,
its tidal pull.

Wednesday, breakfast. Rain in staves.
Too shy to meet the other's eye,
our fingers touch by the tea cosy,
sweet peas in a jar.

On Thursday the sun broke through,
drawing steam from potato fields.
Hand in hand we strolled downstream
from Wormingford to Wissington

and lay in the graveyard by the church
where an ancient painted dragon lurks.
Knot-grass, harebells,
clumsy bumble bees.

It's dawn – the moon is full again.
The ache of his not being here. I've stripped
the cow, she saunters off. Blue silk
riffles the cooler's ribs.

First the clink of empty churns
then a rumble within my breast.
Forty bombers thundering east,
heavy with their deadly load.

Brave boys those, so far from home!
But where is he? Tunisia, France?
As I shade my eyes and watch them go,
his child quickens for the very first time.

Anne Boileau

En Souvenir de Vercors

Always, when I peel Jerusalem artichokes,
wash off the mud, reveal their alien grotesqueness,
I am shifted to a dank day forty years ago.
Across the room, in an apartment in Valence,
a dark-haired teacher's sitting in a bucket chair,
her head in profile in the lamp's half light.
Lent's approaching and she's offered us *beignets*.
Somehow artichokes, *les topinambours,*
become our conversation as we two English say
we haven't seen them in the shops in France.
Her wan face twists, she gives a tiny shudder,
but then recalls herself. Looking straight ahead,
she explains with no emotion, pedagogically,
that in the Vercors, in the war,
there was little else to eat.
Her family avoids them now or feeds them to the pigs.
But it is clear she hates them for the memories
that spring so strong, that their misshape
and powerful taste bring back.

Ever since, I pare the knobbles with the greatest care
so that I waste as near to nothing as I can;
in tribute to the mothers, wives and daughters
of the maquisards betrayed in summer forty-four.

Diana Hirst

Judith Lunn *Earth*

(left) Sarah Lidster *The Bends*

Maria Medina Inglesias *Landgirl's Song*

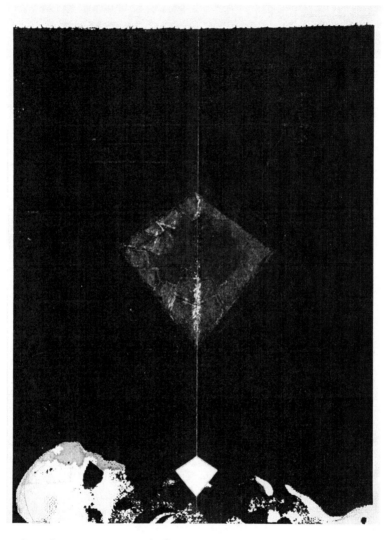

Abigail Ryman *No End of a Lesson*

(left) Arlene Machin *A Ballad of 2014*

*His missing leg eats kidneys
for breakfast...*

His Missing Leg

Is quite blasé
Is one of God's chosen limbs
Dreams of phantom ships
Marches through Georgia

His missing leg eats kidneys for breakfast
Gambles on rouge and impair.
Prays for the community of scrap metal
Lolls in the back room, ready for the fun run

His missing leg fires on all four cylinders
Usually comes from behind
Sifts the grass for the missing gem
Leaves a dent on the hassock

His missing leg will put you at your ease
Darns socks in the desert evenings
Lifts up its eyes unto the hills
and dimly views the prosthesis

His missing leg has tricks up its trouser
Steps right up to the line
Wouldn't consent to be used as a squinch
Always pays for his round.

His missing leg trips on Awayday Specials
Sends postcards to his mum
Spells his name backwards to amuse the kid in the pew
Lights candles in his brain every day

Josh Ekroy

Extraordinary Rendition

This man is dangerous.
He breathes ideas that spread unease.
He makes accomplices
like secret clusters of infection,
pools of poison – needing
to be drained with needles,
knives, before they breed a fever.

His attitude to death
is so obscene he looks ahead
to visualise his own as if
he disbelieves or fails
to understand finality.
He'd approach an open grave
as if unshocked by putrefaction.

If he disapproves
of us then he is free to go
elsewhere. He cares so much
about Samaritans, so let him
settle in Samaria!
If not we'll give him up to hands
less hand-tied than our own. And they
can settle with him as they please.

Michael Bartholomew-Biggs

The Bolshevik

Your eyes are drawn
to my hands. Each one
could cover your face.
Thick-fingered and
knuckle-gnarled,
they worked until they bled
and cracked like the land.

These hands swung
an axe, split hard wood
as if it were soft sand.
Strange how gently they hold
this banner of blood.

My booted legs are
thick trunks rooted
in a forest of tiny people.
Am I real? I think
they have made me
in their own image.

Your eyes meet
my hawk-eyes
that do not waver.
They look beyond and above
the snow-crusted trees,
the dome-glittered city.
The banner of blood
flutters and blows.

Karen Dennison

'No End Of A Lesson' *from Part 11*

'We have had no end of a lesson: it will do us no end of good.'
Rudyard Kipling, 'The Lesson'

You have seen the photographs, of course –
All skulls and eyeballs, bodies like bundles of bones
Cackhandedly wrapped in skin?

No, you have not seen them.
You have seen pictures *like* them.
The Boers of the Transvaal and the Orange Free State

Could know nothing of Belsen or Ravensbrück
Still to come, forty years down the road:
Only the designs of early British camps

Where mothers, wives, young children
In this and thirty others
Died off quickly in the heat at Christmas,

Or the freezing rains of the high veld in July –
Not forgetting, as we usually do, all the other camps
For the servants and labourers

Who were not white. They were dying too –
The invisibles in their thousands.
And what was it all for, this 'regular sort of picnic',

This final 'gentleman's war', this 'tea-time' squabble
That became a bath of blood for the new century
To learn how to swim?

Gold, of course. Isn't it always gold or
Diamonds or reserves of oil – whatever it takes
To bankroll a ravenous empire with the muzzles off?

Unless you want to say it's competing gods,
Making us mad again and again,
In the same and different ways.

Rodney Pybus

Poor Mohammed's Daughter

Mohammed's fillings, buccal and occlusal
In gaping mouth, when he throws back his head
Confirm the diligence of Baghdad dentists
If not the fact his little daughter's dead
This picture of the grocer is unusual
His howling anguish, shock and disbelief
The intimacy, wedded to intrusion
A war allows us windows on such grief

In eastern England now, the spring advances
A sharp east wind still nibbles at the days
In Colchester, the soldiers' pubs stay empty
As field-by-field the farmland turns to baize
The rooks are building higher, which enhances
The chance that summer comes up with the goods
The sergeants' wives must exercise the dogs now
They hear the transport planes above the woods

A gung-ho newsman on the television
In self-important bullying semi-dark
With barely-bridled relish, talks of tactics
Astride a giant model of Iraq
A line of virtual tanks take up position
And flash up gold explosions on attack
If science can put missiles through a cat-flap
It won't bring poor Mohammed's daughter back

In Babylon, they've cluster bombs not towers
In Nineveh, not quinquereme but Bradley
Where hope dissolves in nausea and migraine
The ancient world is doing rather badly
The children of the modern world spend hours
With drips in arms and bandages on heads
And 'surgical' are strikes – which does seem clearer
Observing tiny patients on their beds

'You betcha melted boots we're coming, mister.
A war is best held fresh or it'll spoil
You gotta go in hard to burst a blister
Especially if that blister's full of oil.'
Poor Mohammed held his daughter, kissed her
Brushed the blood and dust from matted hair
Noting that her body seemed much lighter
Never seeing the camera clicking there.

Martin Newell

Boxers at an Exhibition

The Last Futurist Exhibition, Petrograd 1915

In the materialist corner
we have Tatlin the slapdash
wearing red constructivist shorts.

And in the spiritual corner
Malevich the meticulous
in black suprematist silks.

It's a bare-knuckle fight
in a makeshift gallery
where theories bounce
off corners
        where icons once hung
manifestos face off chin to chin
the crowd is baying for blood on canvas.

Odds are even, they square off:
Vladimir Tatlin, tall and stringy
rooster on barbed wire,
he's starved himself for weeks
living on paint fumes and sawdust
but his timing's all shot,
he's cock-eyed with jealousy.

Kasimir Malevich, seven years older
bulky as a *boyar*, seven years better
at baiting and besting,
swings his ego at the heavens
with infinite confidence.
His tongue takes off
like a flock of albino pheasants
screeching the merits of pure spirit
but his temper burns holes
in his own manifestos.

Tatlin, his arms loose in their sockets,
throws a left-jabble-dart at the giant and crows,
'Where's your social utility now, Kas?'
then a right-hook-a-took and jeer:
'Hey old man, how about a square black eye
in the far corner of your face?'

Malevich doesn't flinch:
powerful as a grizzly
he sweeps Tatlin to the floor
with one blow, the crowd roars,
Tatlin struggles upward,
tightens his ankles,
locates his feet.

No one dares to referee
until a swish of silk and perfume
glides between rooster and bear:
yes, it's Alexandra Exter, she
prises them apart. The crowd boos
but her oxblood pumps claim the floor
with a blinding shine. Her bias-cut dress,
its black-and-white stripes a danger flag
rippling over torso and hips, slices off
all arguments at the knees.

When she declares
the bout over, it's over;
the exhibition closed, it closes.

Nancy Mattson

Unwanted

I am so close,
smell the sore,
iron-gorged earth.
Bated, on the brink
my voice will carry
no trace of subterfuge,
for now, we must advance.

I am not cheerful,
although it is
an engagement of sorts.

Out here in the middle,
we remain dug-in.
As one perished in my arms,
I carry this ruptured vessel
into the desert myself,
and scoop out the grave,
a teacup at a time.

No need to be careful,
we have rules:
the enemy does not obey.

While backs are turned
I strike camp,
slight as a hiccup
I have slipped away,
beyond the reach
of enemy or tyrant
or evil-smelling, cantankerous sores.

I am no longer fearful
for this ill-considered land
we've wrangled.

A congested cough
will hide their grief,
a folded flag
is passed between
a daughter's will,
a lover's tears
and those bowing, gathered heads.

Do not be tearful,
I am not torn,
I have found peace.

Miles Negus-Fancey

When the Buddhas of Bamiyan Fell

for one heart-shocking moment
before the censor kicked in
it was satisfying as the slow collapse

of a factory chimney – or earth falling off
her axis, as you know she will.
Our lips flickered,

a little replica of that great bald fragment
of smile that lies in the valley dust.
Why did they fire their rifles,

shout with glee at wounded trickles
of rock while a watching child
clapped his hands? I remember my mother

once lay, a sleeping giant in the moonlight,
her inscrutable limbs sculpted in silver.
Had I known DEAD

I would have sent its hot golden bullet
straight from my cot to her heart. Not gods
anymore, the Buddhas of Bamiyan,

made part of our own flesh by the long fuse of hate.
Now in our sorrow, none the less true
for being late,

we must carefully bend to our task, piece
together all the shattered Mummies and Daddies,
the Humpty Dumpties, foolish or wise,

finding a kind autumnal patience,
which after that first small greedy lick of pleasure,
may come to us if we wait.

Kate Foley

Mosque in Kabul – 2002

They feed the birds with crumbs from their tables
or grain from late-summer lands
gleaned before the plough sets in
– women whose eyes cannot reveal their sympathies
smoking soldiers lounging with their guns
children, newly walking, ecstatic at mosque doves
who coo before the call to prayer
in the yard before the building.
Thus the birds multiply as at *hajj*
when pilgrims gather at the holy stone
to touch the dextrous hand of God
so numerous as to form a universe
circling with infinitude.

But the Taliban have come to stop the waste:
they'll not let deprivation last
when there's food for base birds.
They'll feed the crumbs to those in unsafe shelters,
spare grain to wasting livestock.
They'll not let pigeons spot the Holy Mosque,
pests soiling the celestial.

Now no one comes with their offerings.
So too have the doves gone – without nourishment.

Antony Johae

This Jerusalem

She has divided her heart. This Jerusalem
builds walls thousands of years wide.
Something snaps, breaks like a thunderclap.
Fissure in rock. This Jerusalem.
A love. A love. Two so precious.
Kiss one and caress the other.
Adulteress. Harlot. The prophets knew you
well.
Blush red with the coming of day.
Your passion is despotic, ripping up roads,
felling olive trees. Love cracks gates,
covers the landscape with craters.
This Jerusalem. Beloved. Desired. Torn in
two.
Blossoms spring through bullet-shot rubble.
Blood red poppies splatter fields.
Her soul lies in pieces. Their souls.
I love you. I love you.
Say it to both, sincerely, in one hour.
Adulteress. Betrayer. This Jerusalem.
She shines in the company of blue skies,
shattering old stone to build new walls,
casting shadows in the valley of Gehenna.
Eternal city, weep amid the fire.
Eternal fire, weep amid the ruins,
where too much love is more terrible
than too little.

Joan Norlev Taylor

Achilles in Helmand

My tent stinks of goatskin. Stuck
here since the Scimitar track
uncogged in the Garmsir fire fight.
The thump of Agamemnon's drum
was a dodgy Chinook blade.
Waited out two hours under fire, then
lifted back to Lashkar Gar.

'Equipment' returned a 'working' tank
which couldn't get into reverse
without restarting the engine.
Drops were a joke, the wrong spares
or none at all.

On leave, Briseis didn't get a rise out of me,
hard to remember
her face in the half light,
the folds of her slip falling.

Volunteered for a second tour.

A quarter of Mastiff armoured vehicles
are out of action as of 00.00 hours
when I come on duty,
suspensions like shitting concrete.

Pte Patroclus and a couple of newly recruited Myrmidons
hit an IED –
a shower of crimson rain across the metal road
at the recapture of Musa Qaleh.

Nothing to do but stare at the Euxine Babes video.

My shield's a reinforced Land Rover,
sand in the carburettor,
graffiti on the nearside door.

Josh Ekroy

Aleppo

I watch her body
Half-mooned in the arms
Of the running man,
Kicking up the dust of Aleppo;
War child, dead child
None of this made sense to her;
The shells, the gun-stuttering,
Tit-for-tat adult stuff...
All they could say
Is that she would be safe,
And so she played on,
Oblivious to the kiss.

And someone
Is carrying a child's body
Draped heavily in his arms,
Blood drying on loosened bandages
Across the opposite side
Of the same Market Square;
Therefore, you'd feel
That today's honours
Are even; that whatever the right,
And whatever the wrong
Both sides have suffered equally,
In innocent death.

At some stage, children
When your mothers have mourned,
Your fathers have been maimed,
Or lowered
Into the Aleppo dust
In rough-cut coffins
One of these armies
Will be declared victor.

But who will feel
Victorious?

Richard Whiting

Overheard in Uz*

When I washed my steps with butter (Job, 29:6)

Those were the days, my friends, my comforters,
when I washed my front steps with butter,
hung all my lamps with gilt lilies
and skipped to the sound of cymbals.

The days when sheep flocked in the streets
and the bright fox fed from my hand each morning;
when there was the scent of mimosa in my hair
and women sold their words in the market place.

They were days of plenty, all right,
days when fountains spouted sparkling wine
and chickens offered themselves for slaughter.
No-one went hungry and our mouths were crammed
with laughter.

Now we weave as worms round village dungheaps,
live with vultures and put our trust in spiders' webs.

Pam Job

* The Land of Uz is generally reckoned to be south of Damascus

On 'the piercing silence of women' *

Well, Pablo, I sit here and try to write,
like you, of wine and conviviality,
about maize, shells, weather, feathers,
anything but those two children in Gaza,
whose faces I can almost see.

The three year old girl, 'with beautiful eyes,'
the doctor said, her arm blown away,
a hole in the back of her head,
not yet dead; the five year old boy with
the base of his spine missing vertebrae.

There is a silence piercing the world.

Holed up here, we are soaked in images,
hear the wails, the sobs, the ululations
of women going to the wells of mourning,
and we are silently screaming
alongside them; can't you see us?

Pam Job

* Pablo Neruda, The Arrival in Madrid of the International Brigades

Postscript

The Standard of Ur*

A chisel-end shaped block of marquetry,
Its comic-strip depicts the wealth and wars,
One either side, of its plump king; ensures
By means of art the right spin on his story:
His size denotes his royal divinity.
Civilisation marching off from Ur
Honours its war-lord with this beauty here –
Red stone, bright shell, blue lapis-lazuli.

Empire to this day wraps up war in stories:
Natural leaders in an epic tale,
The true religion and the chosen race,
The best seductive ideologies;
But art, a double-edged and useful tool,
Buils up some clear-cut arguments for peace.

Julia Brady

* No. 12 in *A History of the World in 100 Objects*,
Neil MacGregor, 2010

Voices

Stephen Boyce (Editor)
Stephen lives in Hampshire. He is a prize-winning poet, published widely in magazines, anthologies and on-line. His collection, *Desire Lines* (Arrowhead Press, 2010) was described as 'intelligent, sophisticated, formally assured .. a truly exciting new voice'. *The Sisyphus Dog* will be published by Worple Press in 2014.

Mike Bartholomew-Biggs lives in London and, with Nancy Mattson, helps organise the Poetry in the Crypt reading series in Islington. He is also poetry editor of the on-line magazine, *London Grip*. His latest collection is *Fred and Blossom*, (Shoestring Press, 2013), a narrative sequence about love and aviation in the 1930s.

Acknowledgements: 'Extraordinary Rendition' appeared in Acumen magazine, summer 1913. 'Tribe' and 'Fault Line's were in 'Tell it Like it Might Be', (Smokestack Books, 2008)

Anne Boileau lives in Essex and at present chairs Suffolk Poetry Society. Her poems have appeared in *Lapidus*, *Artemis*, *Twelve Rivers*, *Poetry Bay New York*, *Orizont Lieterar Contemporan* and several Suffolk poetry anthologies. In 2012 she won 2nd prize in the Crabbe Poetry Competition. She is a founder member of Camden Mews Translators and has translated the German poets Hans Magnus Enzensburger and Georg Trakl among others.

Julia Brady moved to Wivenhoe, Essex on retirement and is a member of Poetry Wivenhoe and Colchester's Stanza group, Mosaic.

Roger Caldwell His latest poetry collection, *Waiting for World 93* (Shoestring Press), has been praised for its variety of perspectives and its global reach. He has also written on philosophy for *Philosophy Now*, on world politics for *Planet* and as critic and reviewer, for the *TLS*, *P.N. Review* and *Poetry Review*.

Acknowledgements: 'Gas' appeared in Poetry (Chicago). 'Moments from a Trench Career' and 'Bad Weather' both appeared in Iota magazine.

David Canning has written poetry since he was a teenager and, after some initial success, has only recently taken up his pen again. He is a member of Colchester Mosaic Stanza group. His poem, *An Essex Parish* is the first in a planned series exploring conflict and its impacts set against the backdrop of Essex's own sometimes violent history, in this case, the murder of the first Christian King of Essex, Sighebert, by Swithelm and the subsequent expulsion of St Cedd from Bradwell on Sea.

Ann Clarke remembers absorbing poetry from her father who recited long narrative poems learned by heart at school. When she was introduced to Keats at the age of 16, poetry seemed the only subject worthy of study. In retirement in Wivenhoe, she is able to pursue this life-long interest via various local poetry groups.

Suzanne Conway has poems in *Poetry Review*, *The North*, *The Rialto*, *Smiths Knoll*, *Ambit*, *Magma*, *The London Magazine* and *Seam*. She is also published in *Newspaper Taxis: Poetry after the Beatles*, and *The Captain's Tower: Seventy Poets Celebrate Bob Dylan at Seventy* (both Seren). She is working on a PhD in Creative writing with Glyn Maxwell.

Karen Dennison has poems published in *South*, *Orbis*, *The New Writer*, *Ink Sweat and Tears*, *South Bank Poetry*, *Poetry Wivenhoe* (Wivenbooks, 2011) and *Heart Shoots* (Indigo Dreams). In 2011 she won the Indigo Dreams Collection Competition and her first collection, *Counting Rain*, was published by them in 2012.

Josh Ekroy has poems published in *The Rialto, Smith's Knoll, Magma* and *The SHOp*; on websites such as *Ink, Sweat and Tears, Poetry Proper* and *Blackbox Manifold,* and in anthologies, *The Best British Poetry, 2011* (Salt). He lives in London.

Acknowledgements: 'His Missing Leg' first appeared on the website Bow Wow Shop. 'Achilles in Helmand' was commended in the Ver Prize 2010 and appeared in their anthology.

Kate Foley was born in London before WW2 and remembers it all too well. Her anthology poem reflects a professional connection with the conservators trying to repair the damage to our necessary icons from more recent conflicts. Her latest collection is *One Window North* (Shoestring Press, 2013).

Caroline Gill co-authored a chapbook, *The Holy Place*, with John Dotson in 2012 (Seventh Quarry, Swansea; Cross-Cultural Communication, New York). She won the International Petra Kenney Poetry Competition (General Section) in 2007. Her poems have been published widely in the UK and beyond.

Mike Harwood has had two plays performed by Colchester Theatre Group. He has read at the Essex Book Festival and the Essex Poetry Festival. His poems have appeared in *Chimera* magazine, *Genius Floored* (2009) and in *KJV: Old Text, New Poetry* (Wivenbooks, 2011). His first collection *Words Count* was published in 2007. He teaches Creative Writing at the University of Essex.

Cameron Hawke Smith wrote poetry in his youth but has only recently started to submit works for publication. He has a degree in Classics and his translations from Pindar, Homer, and Horace, as well as Rilke and Sorley MacLean, have appeared in *Modern Poetry in Translation* and *The Guardian*.

Diana Hirst grew up in East Kent within sight of the French coast at a time when both French and English landscapes were healing after six years of conflict. Deal and Dover Poet of the Year in 2008, her poems have also been recognised in the Canterbury Festival, Suffolk Poetry Society and Poetry Wivenhoe competitions.

Pam Job helps organise Poetry Wivenhoe and is a member of Colchester Mosaic Stanza poetry group. She won the Fakenham Poetry Prize in 2010 and Third Prize in 2013. She won the Crabbe Poetry Prize in 2013. Her poems appear in *Artemis*, *Poetry Wivenhoe* collections, (Wivenbooks 2008, 2009) and *KJV: Old text, New Poetry* (2011) and in *From the City to the Saltings* (Essex Poetry Festival, 2013).

Antony Johae divides his time between Colchester and Lebanon, from where his wife comes. He has taught Literature In England, Ghana, Tunisia and Kuwait. His poem, *Mosque in Kabul*, is drawn from a recently completed collection, *Poems of the East*. Work is now progressing on *Lines from Lebanon*. He is also working on *Home Poems* and a collection dedicated to the French film director, Eric Rohmer, *After Images*.

Oliver King was a prizewinner in the 1996 W.H.Smith Young Writers' Competition. He then studied Creative Writing at UEA and is now working on a PhD at Essex University. His work appeared in *Creel* (Univ. of Essex) and he won the Essex Book Festival Short Story Competition in 2013.

Neave Lynes is thirteen years old and wrote *The Deserter* in her Year 8 English class at St. Helena School, Colchester. She enjoys writing poetry and having had her poem selected for this anthology, she has started writing more in her spare time.

Petra McQueen is a writer and teacher living in Essex. She has won competitions with her fiction, and her stories and poems have been published in the UK and abroad. Her life-writing has been featured in *The Guardian* and in *You* magazine.

Nancy Mattson moved from the Canadian prairies to London in 1990. Her third poetry collection is *Finns and Amazons* (Arrowhead, 2012). Her first, *Maria Breaks Her Silence* (1989), was shortlisted for the Gerald Lampert Award. Her second collection is *Writing with Mercury* (2006). She co-organises the popular Poetry in the Crypt reading series at St Mary, Islington.

> *Acknowledgements: 'Matt Breaks his Silence' was published in 'Maria Breaks her Silence', (Regina: Coteau Books, 1989). 'Boxers at an Exhibition' was published in 'Finns and Amazons'.*

Adrian May is a songwriter, poet and essayist. His books include *Myth and Creative Writing* (Routledge, 2011) and two collections of poems and lyrics from Wivenbooks, who will also publish his forthcoming book/cd combination, *Comedy of Masculinity*.

Gill Napier has been writing poetry for almost fifty years and has had poems published in *Smith's Knoll* magazine and in *My Mother Threw Knives* (Second Light). Her poems have been commended in the Crabbe Poetry Competition and in 2011, her poem *Golden Wedding* won 1st Prize.

Miles Negus-Fancey has been a decorative artist for thirty years but his daughter reminded him how much he loved to write. This is his first published piece. Wilfred Owen and Siegfried Sassoon turned him on to poetry forty years ago and they both still thrill and amaze him.

Martin Newell is a poet and rock musician. First published in *The Guardian* in 1984, he wrote poems regularly for *The Independent* titles for fifteen years before becoming resident poet for *The Sunday Express* and Saturday columnist for the *East Anglian Daily Times*. In 2010 he won Columnist of the Year Prize at the Eastern Media Awards. He has published a dozen collections of verse, two social histories, a collection of his *East Anglian* columns and a rock memoir, *This Little Ziggy*. He has broadcast widely on national and regional radio and television.

Joan Norlev Taylor has written two novels, *Conversations with Mr. Prain* (Melville House, 2006/2011) and *Kissing Bowie* (Seventh Rainbow, 2013) and a historical travel narrative *The Englishman, the Moor and the Holy City* (Tempus/History Press, 2006). She has co-edited three poetry collections with Wivenbooks including *KJV: Old Text, New Poetry* (2011). Her poetry has appeared in literary journals and collections in her native New Zealand and the U.K.

Rodney Pybus has lived in Suffolk for thirty years. He has published seven collections of poetry and has poems included in the Suffolk anthology *By the North Sea* (Shearsman, 2013). His poems have been translated into French, Spanish, Russian, Czech and Romanian, and set to music in France and England. *No End of a Lesson* is the middle section of a poem in 3 parts, located in the village of Irene near Pretoria. The poem reflects on war in the twentieth century including the Boer War. The full poem appears in *Darkness Inside Out* (Carcanet/NorthernHouse, 2012).

Fran Reader has enjoyed writing and reading poetry for over fifty years and since her retirement has been able to give more time to both and share with other poetry lovers at the Suffolk Poetry Cafés, Browsers' and Arlington's.

Peter Sandberg discovered beauty in the rhythm of words studying Classics at school, learned accuracy in the use of words as a lawyer and the value of the spoken word as a clergyman. He is a regular reader at Sudbury Poetry Café. He was Commended in the 2010 Crabbe Poetry Competition.

Rosie Sandler writes poems, short stories and novels. Her poems have been published in a number of print and on-line anthologies and journals including *The Rialto*, *The Illustrated Popshot Magazine*, *Lighthouse* and *London Grip*. She has a poem in the forthcoming Penguin anthology, *The Poetry of Sex*.

Bryan Thomas started writing poetry in his early twenties but for many years his work was the very opposite of 'emotion recollected in tranquillity'. It is only recently that he has regressed.

Alex Toms has had work published in magazines, journals and anthologies including *Writers' Forum*, *Artemis*, *Poetry South*, *Small Word*, *Reflections from Mirror City* and *Poetry Wivenhoe* (2011). In 2012 she was runner-up in the Essex Poetry Festival Competition. This year her poem, *Becoming Sei*, was Highly Commended in the London Poetry Competition. She writes when her younger son will allow her and she is working towards her first collection.

Richard Whiting has written poetry for as long as he can remember and enjoys the Poetry Aloud group in Bury St. Edmunds. He has a life-long love of rock music and is still a serial 'gigger' at forty eight. He rates Ian Brown of The Stone Roses as amongst the finest poets this country has produced.

Judith Wolton was placed second in the first Poetry Wivenhoe poetry competition and Commended in the Suffolk Crabbe Competition, 2011. Her poems have appeared in the second Poetry Wivenhoe collection, *London Grip*, *French Literary Review* and *From the City to the Saltings* (Essex Poetry Festival Antholgy, 2013). She is a member of Colchester Stanza group, Mosaic, and is on the committee of Suffolk Poetry Society.

Acknowledgement: 'French Harvest' appeared first in French Literary Review.

Lightning Source UK Ltd.
Milton Keynes UK
UKOW04f0045270314

228883UK00005B/60/P